Acrylic Painting for Newbie's

Your Easy Path to Artistic Expression

Courtney   James

Table of Contents

CHAPTER ONE

INTRODUCTION

These reusable paper paint ranges are obviously huge for keeping cleanup I've used them, and they get cleanup moving quickly. Picking a surface for acrylic painting is a briskness step since there are so many surfaces acrylics can work wonderfully on. Most of engineered materials have forever been built from material that has been joined over a wooden edge and got with bunk bars rearward to guarantee their legitimacy. You can now look at different surfaces, including shakes, level material, paper, and sheets of wood. Painting your walls is another astonishing surface that is overall ignored.

TIP #1: Get a set material. Essentially a material's been painted (or prepared) with gesso and is prepared for acrylic paints out of the pack. Notwithstanding, vast them are made under the brand name only for approval. Gesso is a base for acrylic painting and considers the paint to float significantly more clear.

TIP #2: Promise you don't buy a material sorted out for oil painting your acrylics will not stick exactly as expected to it. In the event that you're learning with acrylics, I these material sheets are a fair choice. They're more reasonable than extended material so you can rehearse your point of view and managed some cash. These material sheets might be outlined for show later on. You can clean your paint and hose brushes with a central cup or holder of water while changing groupings and hurting them for easier application.

Star tip:

A framework that can't be envisioned and can't be stayed away from is two cups of water. Wash the brush with one cup of water after each party; One cup to use to debilitate paint and hose brushes when required. Void the cup and flush it with clean water when the water becomes "faint." It's also prudent to have a paper towel on hand in case there is too much water. Get an easel (discretionary) Paying little psyche to what the way that you shouldn't quickly play with an easel as a juvenile, it will in general perceive a squeezing part if you truly have any desire to paint upstanding. The advantage of an easel is that it sets your material up as a point which strikingly assists with viewpoint, piece, and degrees. While I'm working with a material, I generally make a section from the easel to truly zero in on my speculation and ensure I'm pushing ahead. I other than flip it over on the easel to see it from a substitute point. Right when your material is level on a table, this requires in a general sense more consistency. Easels vary in their conditions and sizes. You can get a tabletop one (you a basic piece of the time see these being utilized at Paint Nite occasions), or you can get a story easel. This convertible easel is my most loved in light of the fact that it very well may be utilized as either a tabletop easel or a story easel, permitting you to pick. Now that we've covered the innovative creation supplies you'll require, you ought to pick a thought of what to paint. It has all of the characteristics of an endeavor that is sufficiently essential, but I notice that it is reliably the most hazardous, especially when you are just start. Consider the level of difficulty. Specifically, you totally need to choose something incredibly quick. You might become surprised and lose interest while traversing that it is unusually risky, which is not what I want for you.

Try a few striking material concepts that have been skillfully painted, however, if you are absolutely certain and require a test. You should choose the proper convincing craftsmanship trouble level to partake meanwhile and be convinced to paint!

ENDEAVOR AN ORGANIZED INSTRUCTIVE NEW TURN OF EVENTS

For some impetus material thought on what to paint, I've worked with an improvement only for you: 71 verifiable contemplations of material craftsmanship. The vast majority of the improvement's evaluations are based on text or video as sources of information. Examine these an additional conspicuous number of key number of than 50 scene painting assessments or these an extra fundamental number of major number of than 40 couple painting practices to spread out scenes obviously to go through a senseless evening getting out and about. If you are responsible for sorting out a paint night, you will track down that this post on taste and painting will help. Youngsters are other than titanic concerning coordinate adolescents. Stoneware painting, uncommon expressive clarifications, and genuine material gems are enormously immense and proper for teenagers' innovative reasoning. To comprehend the cycle, in case you have never painted, you could need to pick your most head relationship from a coordinated video practice.

What to Paint: Evaluations for free-form painting without a planned improvement If planned practices don't work for you, two or three more options are taking several tests. Taking into account standard normal presence motivation:

1. Sprout you filled in your garden jar   of blossoms

2. You're inclined toward indoor plant   a bowl of standard thing (or individual standard things)

3. Direct scene

4. your central unpredictable things an immense latte craftsmanship or mug of coffee   still life objects you have at home (cups, bowls, bottles, and so on.)

5. The ocean side nursery

Moving beyond generally for the ceaseless that you're painting without an edifying turn of events, promise you read through the "Party the Connection" piece under before you get everything going. On the off chance that you began with a piece of craftsmanship, you ought to begin painting the material immediately. Having said that, placing an additional step into your adornments before you start can cause it to seem more appealing and more satisfying to the eye.

The particular work you really will not have any impact expecting that you've set yourself up in a manner for hosed question right all along. It will comparably assist you with jumping further into acrylics and signs all over. Unfortunately, in spite of being an adequately clear exhibition or rule, it is much of the time overlooked, and now and again, it is even not showed in workmanship classes.

What's going on?

"The norm of the thirds" is facilitated. In general, when painting a point (such as sprouts, scenes, a bowl of ordinary things, etc.), you should use the "rule of thirds." A pencil ought to be utilized to draw your plan first. This will help you with better investigating the creative methodology as it advances, and all that will remain in fundamental level. While making dynamic work, remember the third rule and apply it near the finish to put focal places where they should be. Noticing Your Work There could come when your acrylic painting doesn't feel exceptionally right. Plus, a principal number of the times, you can't pinpoint what screwing with you since you have been checks out at your material with a near viewpoint. Your eyes can't "see" what is leaving interest, regardless of whether you have been involved for quite a while. paint expecting that they truly dry on.

CHAPTER TWO

UTILIZING ACRYLIC PAINT IN A PROTECTED MANNER

Acrylics are normally exceptionally protected to utilize, yet some of them can be unsafe on the off chance that not dealt with as expected. Additionally, just to put things in setting, colors are more stuffed in capable level paints and lesser in student quality ones.

1. Know about the accompanying assortments:

2. Cadmium tones

3. Cobalt course of action tones

Despite what the variety, coming up next are a safeguarded ways of managing dealing with a paint, so that you're inclined to fittingly use them:

1. Wash hands totally with water and manufactured after use

2. Manage without eating/drink while painting

3. Keep paint out of eyes, mouth, and lungs

4. Use eye confirmation expecting your finishing something like splatter painting

Other than with all craftsmanship material, get paints a long way from little children.

Young understudies should be seen and shown safe managing techniques. Assuming that no one will notice that you are looking for safe acrylics for young people, check the paint bottles for the "Embraced Thing" seal.

FINDING THE RELISH THE EXPERIENCE OF PAINTING

An Overseeing oneself Structure

Right when you at first get painting in a really drawn out time frame, other than with administering any new skill, it can transmit an impression of being surprising. Moreover, every so often when things don't turn out to be precisely true to form, it can get a piece upsetting. Your expressive expressions presumably won't turn out how you figure they will the secret for the most part on different events. I never would have discovered the joy that comes from painting with acrylics if I hadn't given up so long ago when I first started out. I have used my remarkable ability to paint in a variety of ways and at a variety of times throughout my daily life. It has been both my treatment as it has my creative outlet. I long for you to accomplish a similar degree of satisfaction through painting. Learn how to empathize with your inner expert and practice self-compassion, and take the necessary precautions to avoid being excessively unforgiving of yourself and your work! I comprehend I've been at fault for being my own most outrageously shocking academic, yet fortunately this can be changed. All that is required is a change in setting (like when you were investigating your acrylic painting). If you are able to do that, you will find that exhibiting art or anything else you do in your day-to-day life is fundamentally extremely appealing. As opposed to whipping yourself considering the way that your specialty seems like you had trusted, shift your fixation to the higher viewpoint thinking about everything: You are valiant to master and practice ability that many individuals fear or don't carve out opportunity to learn. Recognize yourself and be content with each ensuing you spend exploring new fulfillments, experiences and eliminating an amazing doorway to place assets into yourself. Watercolor versus Acrylic Paint Various amateurs much of the time inquire, "Is acrylic painting more straightforward than watercolor painting?" The short reaction is acrylics are significantly clearer for teenagers. While watercolor and acrylic paints are similar in that they are both water-soluble and easy to clean up, painting with watercolor can be very specific and requires more practice to learn and change the color and amount of water used. Some instructors even recommend that their students take a few classes in acrylics before moving on to watercolor. Assuming that you truly want to paint with watercolors, this post on watercolor painting considerations will help you with starting.

SPECIALISTS SUGGEST ACRYLIC PAINT OVER OIL PAINT

One notable paint is oil paint. In any case, expecting you've whenever worked with oil paint, you comprehend how testing it will overall be. Fortunately, you can drop by an especially like result using Acrylic. However, if you're still not convinced, we should go over two or three distinctions between oil paint and acrylic painting.

Acrylic Paints can be changed into clear (watercolor-like) by debilitating it with water or used in a smooth weak consistency like oil paints. Like oil paints, acrylic paints can be joined to make various assortments, covers, and combinations. Oil paint can be applied over dried acrylic paint, but oil paint cannot be applied over acrylic. Stood apart from oil paints, acrylic paints are more sensible. For not an incredibly clear explanation expressly. Might you at whatever point ultimately tell which painting under is painted with Oil paints and which one is painted with acrylic paints?

CHAPTER THREE

PAINTING OF A COLDER SEASON SCENE

Colder season Scene with a Winding Street and Mountain Scene It's attempting to tell isn't it? Because of their comparative cloudy characteristics contrary to "straightforward," the two paints can measure up to each other. You definitely still should fathom which can't do whatever it takes not to be which, right? Oil paints were used to arrange the principal picture, which depicts the lodge and curving street during the cooler months. The second imaginative creation's mountain scene was painted with acrylics. After working specifically with each of the three paint mediums, I truly believe that acrylic paints are the best option for beginners. In any case, the assumption to learn and adjust for oils and watercolor paints is hardly more limit than for watercolors in light of multiple factors. As periodically as conceivable Presented Requesting about Acrylic Painting

WHAT MATERIALS FORCE UP ACRYLIC PAINT?

Acrylic paints are fast drying paints produced using different fixings that are consolidated in a polymer medium a material that is like plastic in its conveyance. Without a doubt, acrylics are water-dissolvable, proposing that they can be decreased and cleaned with water. However, once dried, they become impervious to water and have a surface made of plastic that is malleable and brittle. Acrylic paints can be used on material, wood, paper, sheets, rocks, and various materials.

HOW MUCH TIME SHOULD ACRYLIC PAINT BE ALLOWED TO DRY

It depends on how thick the paint is. A slight layer of acrylic dries in an issue of a short period of time, while thicker strokes of paint can require a couple of additional minutes. Nevertheless, not in any way shape or form like oil syntheses, which can dry absolutely in three to a half year, this isn't correct. How is it that acrylic could paint be concealed, say, an old synthesis that ought to be reused? At whatever point made by workmanship has near no surface to it, you could from an overall perspective at any point conceal it with a coat or two of white Gesso (acrylic starter). If there are stacks of surface (made by craftsmanship isn't level or smooth to the touch), you ought to sand it down a piece going prior to applying the layers of Gesso. Moreover, acrylic paint will strip or sever whenever applied over oil canvases.

ACRYLIC PAINTS ARE A FANTASTIC DECISION FOR AMATEURS

Since acrylics are so widely used, a number of experts have deemed them to be the most "smart" of the paints. How might I give my acrylic painting more shine? In case you're attempting to get sheen over your entire synthesis, read the part above about fixing your material. Be that as it may, assuming your goal is to clean only one piece of your work of art (for example Paint and a medium should be joined in the event that you want to paint a lake. Adding a smidgen of shimmer medium to your paint is the most direct strategy for achieving that brilliance. The medium will thin the paint and make it require greater investment to dry. Paint mediums are irrefutably not an infuriating procedure for adolescents, yet they're not difficult to utilize. Acrylic craftsman's have been known to incorporate a wide variety of materials into their paint, for instance, espresso beans and eggshells, to achieve a particular surface or grow the drying time for additional created handiness. I go into a lot of detail in My A-Z Acrylics for Juveniles if you really want to learn about mediums. For students who need to assess paint parts bizarrely, I would overwhelmingly propose Astonishing juvenile's outline of Acrylic mediums. I purchased this set for myself, and I love it. Six holders of outstanding mediums are incorporated for your testing. Might I at whatever point utilize acrylic paint to paint rocks or various materials? While material or thick paper is typically utilized as a show-stopper surface in different acrylic paint instructive exercises, there are different choices. A few contemplations are:

1. Rocks

2. Water bottles

3. Stoneware creation;

4. Wood cuts

5. Ornaments of plastic

GLASS COMPARTMENTS PAINT ON WATER CONTAINERS

One endeavor I completed two or three months earlier was to paint water bottles that could be reused. The water bottles were given to me as Christmas presents, however they would comparatively make intriguing presents for Mother's Day and birthday celebrations! Enduring basically until additional notification that you're looking for some exceptional occasion painting considerations, take a gander at this Christmas painting thoughts blueprint.

HOW TO PAINT ON ROCKS

Another on-plan/extraordinary material acknowledged is rock painting. Rock painting is a fun, effective, and simple activity that is suitable for adults as well as young people. All you truly need is a stone/rock, some acrylic paint, and some inspiration! Take a look at my comprehensive Stone Game plan 101- Crazy Aide to learn the fundamentals of rock painting. This 141 stone material contemplations post will move you to paint your generally imperative stone whenever you have all that you need. Is it genuine that you are searching for extra youngster cordial artwork thoughts? This 83 kids painting considerations post has flood examinations for your young making arranged specialists. Likewise, since it is currently your move, you have a strong comprehension of the essentials of acrylic painting. I'll give it to you immediately.

What will you include in your brand-new beginning?

In the occasion you have new beginning fear, you can check out at a piece of my immediate acrylic educational activities here. I would like to know what kind of painting you will create, so please leave a comment below and share your thoughts. You might inspire another talented artist. Guessing that your dying ought to learn anything explicitly with Acrylic pieces, let me know and I'll guarantee I cover it (either here or another).

CHAPTER FOUR

FUNDAMENTAL ACRYLIC PAINTING TIPS FOR NOVICES

Could you say you are ready to endeavor acrylic painting anyway dubious where to start? Then again maybe you have actually started painting regardless essentially need a couple of pointers. Acrylics are excellent for newborns. They are really easy to use, dry quickly and are more sensible to buy than oils or watercolors. You can get everything rolling with acrylic painting and partake in the process by following a few fundamental tasks.

Acrylic Paint

1. Instead of making your own paint, use paint of a good quality if you can afford it. There are numerous brands available at various prices. Paint in the proficient grade has more assortments and will make it simpler for you to mix and focus harder. Besides, an enormous part of basic brands offer fair paints for understudies that are fitting for youngsters.

2. Acrylic paint is quick to dry, This can be heavenly to acknowledge that a layer will dry, which you would have to do with oil paint, yet it might be really jumbling when you genuinely need to blend. While

working with acrylics, it's ideal to work rapidly or utilize an extender that ought to accelerate the drying system.

3. Sort out a suitable technique for mixing tones. If you sort out some way to mix your own assortments and shades, you will really need to save cash and broaden your reach. From the three fundamental tones red, blue, and yellow you can blend any tone.

4. You can get familiar with collection blending by perusing my post on the arrangement hypothesis. Sort out some way to work a collection wheel. Acrylic paint usually dries possibly more dark. Due to the fact that paint contains more

filler rather than as much variety, the more reasonable the paint, the slower it will dry.

5. Buy essential tones, at any rate. Regardless, red, blue, yellow, faint, white, and an unmistakable tint, for example, consumed umber is great. You can mix various blends as critical to. You will finally find which colors you utilize the most, and you can buy those. Starter sets in paint made arrangements for understudies, like this one from Liquitex, are regularly accessible.

6. If you are using the more sensible workmanship type paints (because of cost or responsiveness) you can have a go at adding a spot of white to make them more obscure. More sensible paints have less

shade and are thusly more clear. White will dial down the paint so you ought to really consider using a barely more faint paint or paint various layers to get the tone you genuinely care about. Store capable worker brushes upstanding to thwart hurt

7. Clean your brushes with delicate cleaning subject matter expert and water after each painting meeting. Dried paint is unfathomably hard to get away from brushes. To keep water from entering the ferrule and conveying the paste, lay your brushes level to dry. Water will likewise make the handle's completion erode and the wood to loosen up. In this manner, never bring down your brushes in water for extended time spans.

For additional information about cleaning your brushes see my post on The Best System for cleaning Brushes.

8. With the fibers looking upward, store your brushes. If they are kept in a container, the fibers may become spread out and bowed. Guarantee they are great and dry and a short period of time later store them bristles up in a compartment or other holder.

9. Conveyed brushes are best for acrylic painting. A brush that is neither too firm nor too delicate is absolutely essential. The brushes shouldn't even mess around with to be extreme; regardless, you ought to avoid the genuine brushes from the

dollar store since they regularly crumble into the paint and shed hair.

10. You basically need a few brushes to begin. Regardless, filbert brushes level brushes with an oval top in one or two sizes are great. In like manner, a more vital level wash brush and a fine detail brush are brilliant to have. These can as frequently as conceivable be bought in sets at a sensible cost that are right now critical for youths. You can foster your collection after a few times and select your main brushes.

11. Blend paint with an arrive at bleeding edge. These are other than unpretentious and easy to use for mixing and painting. (Look at my article on the most effective

way to utilize an Arrive at sharp edge). In case you don't have an arrive at sharp edge, you can use a plastic sharp edge, an old Visa, or even a craftsmanship stick.

12. Genuinely make an effort not to balance yourself with others. You are unfamiliar with your craft cycle and strength. It is off track to yourself to balance your persuading compelling artwork with someone who has been painting for quite a while. Genuinely do whatever it takes not to balance your beginning with someone else's middle. You'll have a point of reference when you date each piece so you can remember and see how far your skills have come over time.

14. Make duplicates of your incredible sight. Pictures give a visual record to you and can be used for virtual redirection posts, online portfolios, and site pages.

15. As you paint, take notes for sometime in the future. Make a note of how you blended colors, what you valued about the synthesis, and where you got your reference photograph or something you learned or saw while you were painting. You can propose back to these notes in future work of art get-togethers.

16. Most show-stoppers can typically be covered with a few coats of gesso to conceal them. Check out at my post on the best way to gesso a material). You can begin again by gently sanding the gesso.

17. Sorting out a decent technique for painting is a long cycle and the more you paint the better you get. Make an effort to paint something consistently, whether it is random shapes or just variety blocks. The more you practice the more beautiful you will become with the brush and paint.

18. Make some partition from your work of art a basic piece of the time. From a distance of two or three feet, you get a predominant view. From a decent distance, the general plan and how well the combinations are organizing are simpler to see.

19. Acrylic on Material Sprinkle your paints with water from a shower holder to keep them away from drying out. To save your

paints wetter for mixing, you can likewise fog your artwork surface. Try to locate a container with a fine haze sprayer to avoid large drops of water. Get more to know reaches and how to keep paint wet in my post on ranges. I utilize a body splash bottle that has been completely cleaned and is unfilled.

ACRYLIC PAINTING TIPS

The fast drying time is moreover not ideal enduring you wind up spilling paint on your garments. To sort out a satisfactory technique for getting acrylic paint out of pieces of clothing this post on the most fit methodology to dispose of acrylic paint

from pieces of clothing has a couple of
signs. You can speed up the drying
process by using a hair dryer on a low
setting if you are truly motivated.

THE END